DAY BY DAY ST[ORIES] of JESUS

Stories by ELIZABETH ASHLEY
Illustrated by C. E. CANEY

PRINTED IN
DEAN & SON Ltd.
52 54 Southwark St.
GREAT BRITAIN
LONDON SE1 1UA

© DEAN & SON, LTD. 1964, 1967
This edition published 1980
0 603 00214 5

First Disciples

TWO fishermen went down to the Sea of Galilee. Their faces were tanned by the sun and the wind; their hands were strong from rowing their boats and from letting out and hauling in the big nets full of fish.

They pushed their boat out from the shore and jumped in. Simon began letting out the big net ready for the fish they hoped to catch.

"Come on, Andrew," he said. "Help me with this net."

But Andrew was not listening to Simon. He was standing in the boat shading his eyes from the glare of the sun.

"Look, Simon," he said excitedly. "There's Jesus walking along the beach."

Simon looked where his brother

pointed, and there, walking along the seashore, he saw the man whom people were beginning to talk about.

"It's Jesus of Nazareth, the new teacher," said Andrew. "Look, he's stopped. He is looking this way. If only . . ."

"Hush, man," said Simon gruffly.

The two brothers stood listening as Jesus called to them across the water.

"Follow me," he said, "and I will make you fishers of men."

"It's us he's calling. He wants us!" exclaimed Andrew, hardly able to believe that this could be happening to them. "Coming, Simon?"

But Simon was already pulling in the net.

"Let's row ashore," he said. "We can fish another day."

As Andrew and Simon hurried across the beach to Jesus, Simon said quietly:

"Fishers of men. I wonder what he means by that?"

But he was pleased that Jesus had asked them to go with him. There were a lot of fishermen out in their boats on this fine morning. Some were already drawing in their big nets full of silvery-coloured fish. Others were just pushing their boats out into the water. Some were busy mending their nets. Andrew and Simon knew some of these men. James and John were in one boat with their father, Zebedee. Jesus knew them, too. As he came towards them he called to them.

"Follow me," he said.

Andrew and Simon waited to see what James and John would do. They saw James and John leave their father in the boat and hurry along the beach to Jesus. They, too, were glad Jesus had called them to follow him.

And that was how Simon (whom Jesus named Peter) and Andrew and James and John became the first disciples of Jesus.

Jesus in the Temple

NOT long after Jesus had called his disciples he went to stay in Capernaum, a little town on the Sea of Galilee. His mother and his brothers were with him, and so were his disciples.

"It is nearly time for the Feast of the Passover," he said one day. "Let us go to Jerusalem."

So they set off on the long journey south. As they travelled Jesus thought about his first visit to Jerusalem when he was only twelve years old. He remembered how he had gone into the temple and talked with the teachers. Now Jesus himself was a teacher.

Jerusalem was crowded when Jesus and his disciples arrived.

"What do you think Jesus will do here?" asked one of the disciples.

"We must wait and see," said another. "Do you remember the wedding in Cana?"

When they entered the temple they found it all in confusion. A lot of tables had been put up and on the tables were piles of coins. Men were sitting there counting out the money to the people who wanted change. In another part of the temple cattle and sheep were being sold by their dealers. There were even pigeons for sale. Everywhere there was noise and confusion. Sheep were bleating, cattle were lowing and pigeons were flapping their wings. Above all the noise people were shouting to make themselves heard.

The disciples waited breathlessly to see what Jesus would do. They could see he was angry.

First he picked up some rope and made it into a whip. Then he began to use the whip to drive the whole lot out of the temple. Every-one was so surprised that soon the dealers were hurrying out of the

temple with their cattle and their sheep. Then Jesus went to the tables where the people were still changing their money. With one quick movement he turned the tables upside-down and sent all the money rolling on to the floor. Then he turned to the pigeon-dealers.

"Take your pigeons out of here," he said. "This is my Father's house and I will not have it turned into a place for buying and selling."

Outside the temple the dealers and money-changers were talking angrily among themselves.

"What right had he to drive us out?" they said. "And who is he to say it is his Father's house?"

But the disciples understood. They knew that the temple was God's house. They were beginning to know quite a lot about Jesus.

Let's Forgive

THE disciples learnt a great many things from Jesus as their teacher. Whenever there was something they could not understand, or some question they wanted answered, they asked Jesus about it.

One day Peter asked him about forgiving others.

"Master," he said, "how often ought I to forgive people when they do something wrong? Would seven times be enough?"

Peter seemed to think he was doing very well if he was as forgiving as that. But Jesus did not think so.

"Not just seven times, Peter," he said. "You must go on and on and on forgiving."

Peter looked thoughtful. He did not know whether he could do that.

"I'll tell you a story," said Jesus. "It will help you to understand what I mean." The disciples liked the stories which Jesus told, and they knew they would learn something about forgiving others from this one.

"Once upon a time," began Jesus, "there was a king, and he had a servant who owed him a lot of money. The king thought it was time the servant paid what he owed, so he said to him:

" 'Pay me what you owe.'

"But the servant had not enough money to do this and he was very worried.

" 'I'm sorry I cannot pay you now,' he said. 'Please give me time and I will pay you all of it.'

"And because the king was sorry for him he told him he need not pay the money at all. But the servant met another servant who owed him money. It was only a small sum—not nearly so much as he owed to the king. But this man who had been treated so well and told he need not pay anything was not willing to do the same to the man who owed him money. He caught hold of him roughly.

" 'Pay me what you owe,' he said.

" 'I'm very sorry,' said the other man. 'I can't pay you now. Please wait a little while and I will pay you all I owe.'

"But the man who had been treated so kindly by the king would not forgive the other man his debt.

" 'You must go to prison until you can pay,' he said.

"When the rest of the king's servants heard about this they went to the king and told him what had happened. Then the king was very angry.

" 'You have been very wicked,' he said to his servant. 'You owed me a great deal of money and I forgave you and said you need not pay it back. You ought to have done the same to your fellow servant. Now you also must be sent to prison until you pay me what you owe.' "

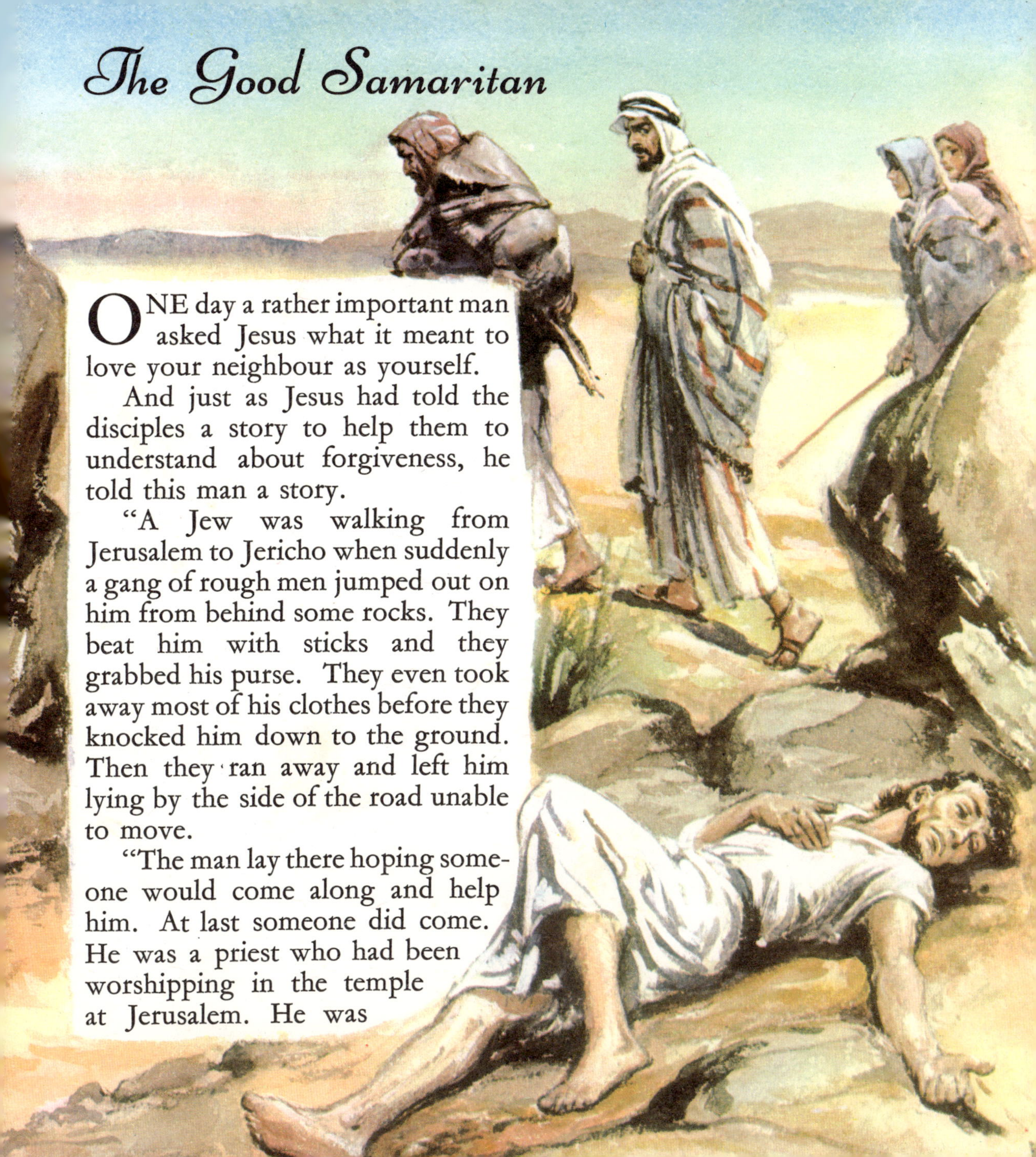

The Good Samaritan

ONE day a rather important man asked Jesus what it meant to love your neighbour as yourself.

And just as Jesus had told the disciples a story to help them to understand about forgiveness, he told this man a story.

"A Jew was walking from Jerusalem to Jericho when suddenly a gang of rough men jumped out on him from behind some rocks. They beat him with sticks and they grabbed his purse. They even took away most of his clothes before they knocked him down to the ground. Then they ran away and left him lying by the side of the road unable to move.

"The man lay there hoping someone would come along and help him. At last someone did come. He was a priest who had been worshipping in the temple at Jerusalem. He was walking on the other side of the road and he looked across at the poor man who was so much in need of help. But he did not go across the road to him.

"Then along came another man. He stopped and looked at the man lying by the roadside. " 'Poor man,' he said, and shook his head. But he went on his way without even trying to help.

"Then at last a Samaritan came along. He was riding on a donkey. The man on the ground did not expect any help from him because the Jews and the Samaritans were not friends. But the Samaritan got off the donkey and went to have a look at the man. He bent over him and said:

" 'Poor man. I'm so sorry. Let me help you.' And he put some oil on his wounds and bandaged them.

" 'Now that's a little better,' he said. 'Let me get you on to my donkey and we'll find somewhere for you to stay and be cared for.'

"So the Jew rode on the donkey and the Samaritan walked beside him. Presently they came to an inn. The innkeeper was surprised to see a Samaritan helping a Jew, but he was still more surprised when the Samaritan said:

" 'Here is some money. I must go on my way now. Will you look after this man and give him what he needs? If you want any more money I will give you some when I come back.' "

When Jesus had finished telling the story he looked at the man who had asked him about loving his neighbour. Then Jesus asked him a question.

"Which of these three men do you think was neighbour to the man who was beaten and robbed?"

"The one who was kind and helpful to him," he said.

"Then," said Jesus, "you go and do the same."

Jesus and the Rich Ruler

AS Jesus became more and more known, all kinds of people came to talk to him. Some came because they were curious. They wanted to know if all the things they had heard about him were true. Others came because they were ill and they hoped Jesus could make them well.

But there were some who came because they really wanted to be helped to live a good life. One of these was a young man who was very rich. He was one of the Jewish rulers, and the more he heard about Jesus the

more he wanted to follow him. Yet he had a feeling that he was not good enough. He thought a lot about this until, one day, he decided to ask Jesus about it.

It was not easy to get to Jesus because there was always such a crowd of people around him. But he pushed his way through the crowd until he got right to where Jesus and his disciples were standing.

"Master," he said, "I want to be good like you. I want to have eternal life. Please tell me what I have to do."

"There is only one who is really good," said Jesus, "and that is God. But I am sure you know the commandments."

And Jesus began to repeat the laws which Moses had made.

"Yes, yes," said the ruler. "I know all those and I have always tried to keep them. But what else must I do?"

Jesus looked at the young ruler and he knew what was wrong with him.

"There is one thing you must do if you really want to have true riches," he said. "You must sell everything you have and give the money to the poor. Then come and follow me."

Now when the young man heard that he was very sorry, because he really wanted to follow Jesus. Yet, although he was so rich, he did not want to part with any of his riches, not even so that he could follow Jesus. He hung his head and walked away without another word.

And Jesus was very sad.

Jesus and the Pharisees

ALTHOUGH so many people crowded round Jesus, they were not all friendly towards him. The Pharisees did not like Jesus at all and they were always trying to find fault with him. They went to the temple regularly and they made a lot of rules about what ought to be done and what ought not to be done, and they thought they were very good people. But Jesus did not think so because they thought more about keeping their rules than about keeping God's laws. Some of their rules were foolish and Jesus did not try to keep them, neither did he encourage his disciples to do so.

One Sabbath morning, when Jesus went into the temple, he saw a man with a useless hand. The Pharisees were waiting to see whether he would heal the man.

"Is it right," asked one of the Pharisees, "to heal anyone on the Sabbath?"

Now Jesus knew that they would say that it was wrong to heal anyone on the Sabbath. He knew, too, that they wanted to charge him with doing something which was against their

rules. But Jesus always did what he knew to be right, whether people liked him or not. But before he healed the man he asked the Pharisees a question.

"Is it right to do good or to do evil on the Sabbath? To save life or to destroy it?"

And the Pharisees could not answer.

Then Jesus turned to the man with the withered hand.

"Stretch out your hand," he said.

That was a thing the man had not been able to do for a long time. But Jesus had told him to stretch it out and he did so, and when he looked at it he found it was strong and useful again.

But the Pharisees were angry with Jesus and they began to plot against him.

Jesus visits his Friends

ONE day Jesus went to visit two of his friends. Their names were Martha and Mary. They lived with their brother, Lazarus, in the little village of Bethany.

It was a surprise visit and only Martha and Mary were in, but they were very pleased to see Jesus.

He sat down, and Mary sat on a low stool beside him. She loved to listen to what he had to say. But Martha thought of all the things which needed to be done. She hurried around tidying up and getting the tea.

As she went about her tasks she could hear the quiet voice of Jesus as he talked to Mary, and one part of her wanted to stop and listen.

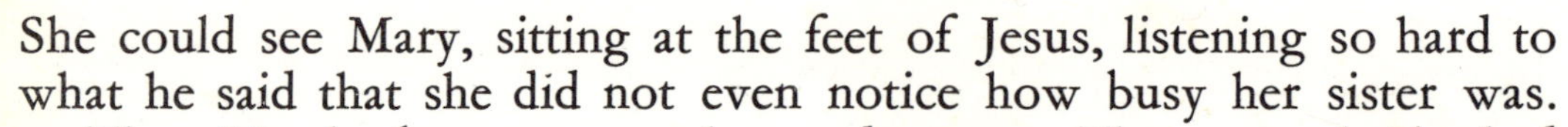

She could see Mary, sitting at the feet of Jesus, listening so hard to what he said that she did not even notice how busy her sister was.

Then Martha began to get hot and angry. The more she looked at Mary, the more cross she became. At last she went to Jesus.

"Jesus," she said, "can't you see that my sister is letting me do all the work while she sits still listening to you? Tell her to come and help me."

Jesus looked up at Martha. He saw her flushed and angry face; then he looked at Mary. She looked calm and happy.

"Martha," he said, "you're fussing too much, and you're fretting about many things which are not important. It would be better for you if you were to do just what Mary is doing —be still and listen.

Jesus and the Children

THE mothers and fathers in Judaea were talking together.

"I hear Jesus is coming this way today," said one mother.

"I know," said another, "and my John wants to go and see him."

"If John is going I'm sure James will want to go too," said another.

"It's not much use taking the children," said someone else. "There is always such a crowd."

"I know what we'll do," said John's mother. "We'll ask everyone to make way so that we can take them to Jesus."

"That's a good idea," said a mother, who had two little girls. "If

our children were to get really close to Jesus they would always remember him."

So they all went home and called their children in from play and told them they were going to see Jesus. At first some of the children were shy and hung back when the crowd moved aside for them. But as soon as they saw Jesus they forgot to be shy. He had such a kind face.

They were very close to him when some of the men who were with him stopped them.

"Take them away," they said to their parents. "Jesus is far too busy to be bothered by children."

Jesus was answering the questions of the grown-ups who were with him. When he saw that the children were being sent away, he said to his disciples:

"Let the little children come to me; do not try to stop them."

Then he called the children, and they ran to him, and he put his arms round them and blessed them.

Jesus and Zacchaeus

THE more Jesus went about preaching and teaching, the bigger became the crowds who wanted to hear him. They followed him everywhere, though some of the people were always trying to criticise and find fault with what he said and did.

One day, when Jesus was passing through Jericho, a very rich man, who lived there, thought he would like to see him. His name was Zacchaeus. He was rich because he cheated and so nobody liked him. When he heard that Jesus was coming, he hurried along the road to meet him. But Zacchaeus was a little man, and the crowd round Jesus was so great that he could not see him at all.

Now Zacchaeus was the kind of man who, if he wanted anything badly enough, kept on trying until he got it. And he did want to see Jesus.

"If only I were taller," he said to himself, and as he said it he looked up.

High above him a sycamore tree flung its branches to right and left, the green leaves giving shade from the heat of the sun. Zacchaeus looked at the tree, and he looked at the crowd which hid Jesus from him. Not since he was a boy had he climbed a tree. He was a rich man now, and rich men did not climb trees. But Zacchaeus could not think of any other way to see Jesus, so, gathering his long robe about him, he climbed up step by step until he reached a strong branch. Then he pushed the leaves aside and looked down. Right below him he could see Jesus, standing in the middle of the crowd.

"Now," thought Zacchaeus, "if only Jesus would look up so that I could see his face."

And at that moment Jesus did look up. He not only looked up, but he saw Zacchaeus and he spoke to him. What he said made Zacchaeus a very happy man.

"Zacchaeus," said Jesus, "come down, for I want to come and have dinner with you."

It did not take Zacchaeus long to climb down again, and soon he was standing beside Jesus, right in the middle of all the people.

"Master," he said, "I have not always done what I should. I am a rich man, but I will give half of all I have to help people in need. Sometimes I have taken more taxes from people than I ought, and I have kept some for myself, but I am going to give back to them four times as much as I have taken from them."

Jesus was happy when Zacchaeus said this.

"I am glad you are sorry for what you have done wrong. Now you are forgiven and can make a fresh start."

God's Loving Care

IT was a beautiful sunny day in Galilee. As Jesus and his disciples walked in the fields the birds were singing in the tree-tops. The fields were gay with all kinds of lovely flowers. Anemones and poppies, tulips and lupins, daisies and lilies were making bright splashes of colour everywhere. Jesus was thinking about God and his love for all these beautiful birds and flowers. But the disciples were talking about what they were going to eat and where they were going to buy clothes.

"Why are you worrying about these things?" asked Jesus. "You must not let yourselves get over-anxious about what you are going to wear or what you are going to eat. God knows that you need these things. If you are always bothering about that you will not be thinking enough

about God and his love for you." Jesus stood still and looked up at the trees where the birds were singing. "Just listen to those birds. They have no store of food, yet God cares for them. And look at all these flowers in the fields and think how wonderfully God has made them. Yet they only live for a few days. If God cares so much about the birds in the air and the flowers in the fields, think how much more he cares for you, for you are of much more value than the birds and the flowers."

"All things bright and beautiful,
All creatures great and small,
All things wise and wonderful,
The Lord God made them all.

Each little flower that opens,
Each little bird that sings,
He made their glowing colours,
He made their tiny wings.

He gave us eyes to see them,
And lips that we might tell.
How great is God Almighty,
Who has made all things well."

MRS. ALEXANDER